COUNTRY · EXPLORERS ·

A Visit to

BELGIUM

By Rebecca Phillips-Bartlett

BEARPORT
PUBLISHING

Minneapolis, Minnesota

Credits

All images are courtesy of Shutterstock.com, unless otherwise specified. With thanks to Getty Images, Thinkstock Photo, and iStockphoto.

Cover – PP Photos, NAPA. 2–3 – TTstudio. 4–5 – Victor-17, max dallocco. 6–7 – QQ7, Pigprox. 8–9 – Sean Pavone, S-F. 10–11 – Rainer Lesniewski, wavebreakmedia, BearFotos. 12–13 – Frans Blok, BeAvPhoto. 14–15 – Tutatamafilm, Botond Horvath. 16–17 – Julian Dael, Kobby Dagan. 18–19 – PeskyMonkey, ShutterOK, Oleksandr Berezko. 20–21 – artjazz, Nina Alizada. 22–23 – Theedi, Wirestock Creators.

Library of Congress Cataloging-in-Publication Data is available at www.loc.gov or upon request from the publisher.

ISBN: 979-8-88509-968-4 (hardcover)
ISBN: 979-8-88822-147-1 (paperback)
ISBN: 979-8-88822-288-1 (ebook)

© 2024 BookLife Publishing
This edition is published by arrangement with BookLife Publishing.

For more information, write to Bearport Publishing, 5357 Penn Avenue South, Minneapolis, MN 55419.

CONTENTS

COUNTRY TO COUNTRY

Which country do you live in?

A country is an area of land marked by **borders**. The people in each country have their own rules and ways of living. They may speak different languages.

Each country around the world has its own interesting things to see and do. Let's take a trip to visit a country and learn more!

Have you ever visited another country?

TODAY'S TRIP IS TO
BELGIUM!

NORTH AMERICA

SOUTH AMERICA

EUROPE

ASIA

AFRICA

AUSTRALIA

Belgium

Belgium is a country in the **continent** of Europe.

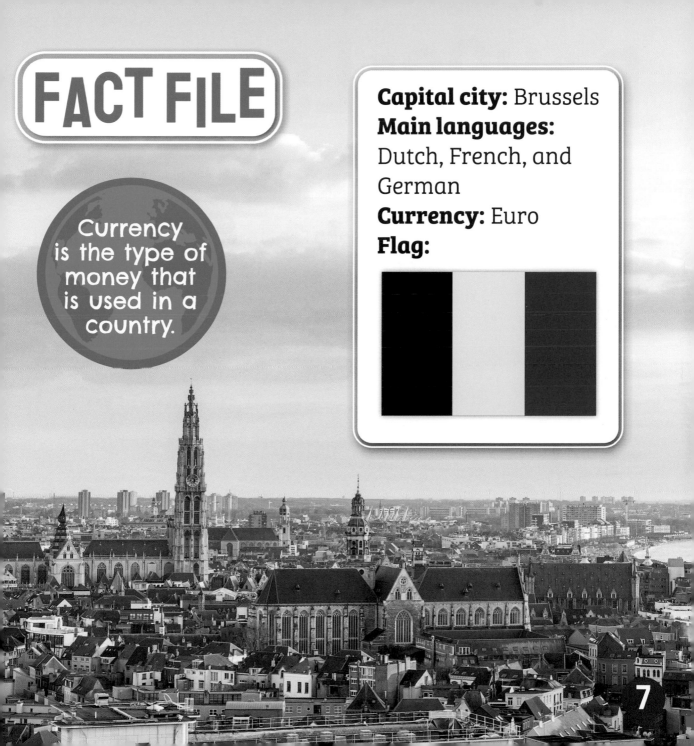

FACT FILE

Currency is the type of money that is used in a country.

Capital city: Brussels
Main languages: Dutch, French, and German
Currency: Euro
Flag:

BRUSSELS

We'll start our trip in Brussels, the capital city of Belgium. Many people call it the capital of Europe. It is a very important city for many countries across the world.

Brussels has more than 120 museums. It is also home to a beautiful old **marketplace** called the Grand-Place.

Parts of the Grand-Place are about 900 years old.

CULTURES

People in Belgium speak many languages. The main language spoken has to do with where in Belgium you are. You may hear Dutch, French, or German.

● Where Dutch is spoken   ○ Where French is spoken   ● Where German is spoken

A handshake is a common Dutch greeting.

Belgium has different **cultures**, too. There are different ways of doing things based on where you visit.

A kiss on the cheek is a French greeting.

THE FOREST IN ARDENNES

Let's head into nature. The Ardennes is a part of Belgium that is covered in forests.

A wild boar

These forests are home to lots of animals. There are wild boars, wildcats, pheasants, and deer.

COMICS

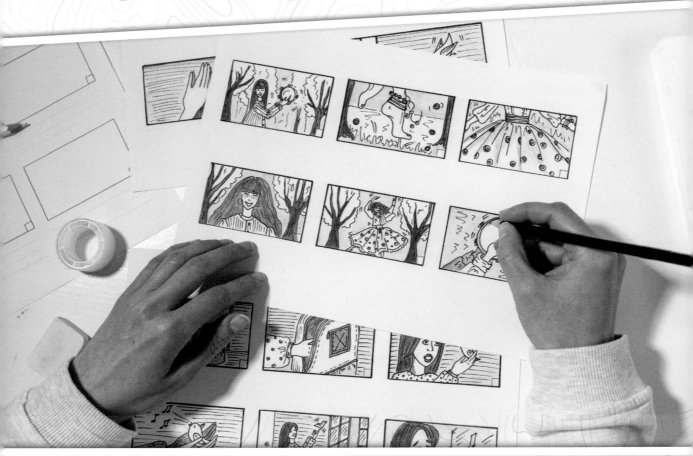

Comics are very important in Belgium. Many famous comics come from here. There are comic **murals** on walls all over the country.

Let's visit Belgium's popular museum all about comics. At the Belgian Comic Strip Center we can see many different comics from history.

FESTIVALS

Tomorrowland Festival

Belgium has many dance and music festivals each year. Tomorrowland is a famous festival that takes place in the town of Boom. It is known for its amazing stages.

The Carnival of Binche is one of the oldest festivals in Europe. It started during the **Middle Ages**.

People dress as a clown called Gilles for this carnival.

FOOD

Which waffle would you try?

Next, let's try some famous Belgian waffles. There are two different kinds. The Brussels waffle is shaped like a rectangle. The Liège waffle is thicker and round.

18

Frites, or french fries, are another popular snack in Belgium. They are usually served with salt and mayonnaise.

THE EUROPEAN UNION

Belgium was one of six countries that helped set up the European Union. This group of countries works together and uses the same kind of money.

The European Union's headquarters is in Brussels. A lot of important meetings happen here.

BEFORE YOU GO

The Atomium

We can't forget to check out the Atomium. This **sculpture** in Brussels is almost 330 feet (100 m) tall. It has been a popular thing to visit for more than 60 years!

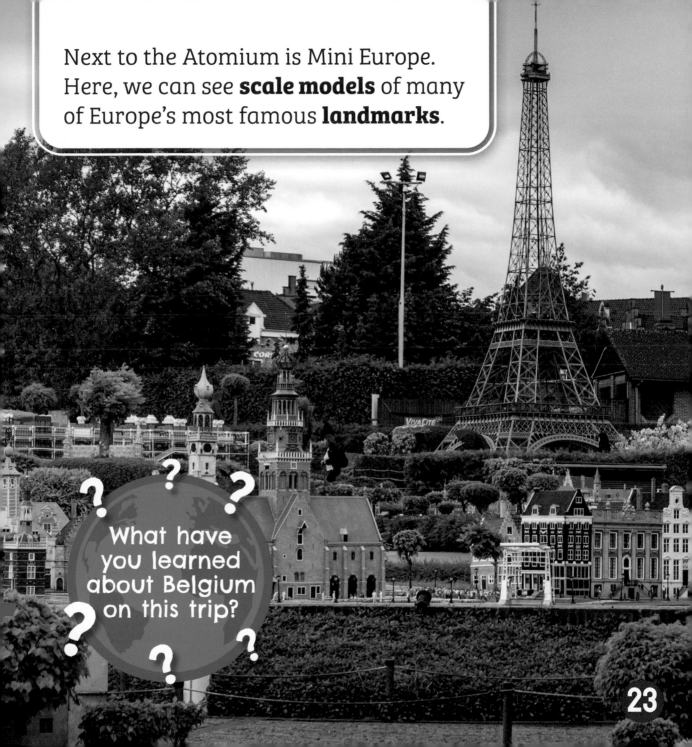

Next to the Atomium is Mini Europe. Here, we can see **scale models** of many of Europe's most famous **landmarks**.

What have you learned about Belgium on this trip?

GLOSSARY

borders lines that show where one place ends and another begins

comics series of drawings that tell a story

continent one of the world's seven large land masses

cultures the traditions, ideas, and ways of life of groups of people

landmarks buildings or places that are easily seen and recognized

marketplace a place where many individual sellers offer their goods for sale

Middle Ages the period of history in Europe from about the years 500 to 1450

murals paintings that cover walls

scale models small exact copies of things

sculpture a statue or other object made by carving or molding marble, clay, or other materials

INDEX